Vegan Mug Cakes

Vegan Mug Cakes

40 easy cakes to make in a microwave

Lottie Covell

K

Photography by Tamin Jones

An Hachette UK Company
www.hachette.co.uk

First published in Great Britain in 2021 by
Kyle Books, an imprint of Octopus Publishing Group Limited
Carmelite House
50 Victoria Embankment
London EC4Y 0DZ
www.kylebooks.co.uk
www.octopusbooksusa.com

ISBN: 9780857839916

Distributed in the US by Hachette Book Group, 1290 Avenue
of the Americas, 4th and 5th Floors, New York, NY 10104

Distributed in Canada by Canadian Manda Group, 664
Annette St., Toronto, Ontario, Canada M6S 2C8

Publishing Director: Judith Hannam
Publisher: Joanna Copestick
Editor: Jenny Dye
Designer: Nikki Ellis
Photographer: Tamin Jones
Production: Allison Gonsalves

A Cataloguing in Publication record for this title is
available from the British Library

Printed and bound in China

10 9 8 7 6 5 4 3 2 1

What is a vegan mug cake?

Simply mix together everyday vegan ingredients in a mug and cook in a microwave to make a delicious cake. Ready in no longer than 15 minutes, with minimal washing up – and in many cases without having to use the scales. Seems like a no-brainer, eh?

Vegan baking isn't the easiest, and in my experience it can be hard to find plant-based recipes that match up to traditional versions. But the microwave comes to our aid here and makes the process fast, simple and fail-safe.

When cooking cakes in a microwave rather than baking them in the oven, the biggest differences are how the heat works and the speed with which it does the job. Ovens bake cakes from the outside in, whereas microwaves work in the opposite way. Although this means we lose the thick outer edge of crumb on the cake, we do keep the desirable soft, fluffy texture inside. I have also found that the intense microwave heat makes the cake batter rise better and set faster, giving a vegan sponge a helping hand, as it lacks the egg that would traditionally serve this purpose.

The challenge with cooking cakes in the microwave is achieving a fine balance: too much heat, and the cake rises too quickly and sinks; too much batter, and it flows everywhere; cook the cake for too long, and it turns out very dry. However, after much testing and trying different variations, I have found the secret to making vegan mug cakes with success every time!

I hope after you have tried out a few of these recipes you will know exactly where to look for a fast, vegan-friendly sweet treat, and once you have gained confidence, you can start experimenting with your own flavour combinations.

The ingredients

EGG ALTERNATIVES

The main role of eggs in a cake is to help raise and stabilise the batter. There are a few vegan egg alternatives that work well in the microwave. I find that potato starch works best, closely followed by cornflour. Potato starch can be bought from online suppliers or health-food shops. If you can't find it, cornflour works almost as well and is much more widely available. Other alternatives include potato flour and ground flaxseeds.

RAISING AGENTS

Baking powder is the main raising agent used in the recipes. After testing self-raising flour and bicarbonate of soda, I found that baking powder provides a good rise that is less likely to collapse. It also has the mildest flavour, which works best with the short cooking bursts of microwave baking.

VEGAN CHOCOLATE

All supermarkets now sell vegan chocolate. Most dark chocolate is made without dairy milk anyway, but make sure you check the packaging. Good-quality vegan white chocolate is a little harder to find. Although some supermarkets do stock it, there is definitely a wider range on offer from health-food shops. There are plenty of options available online, providing you with a perfect excuse to try them all out!

CACAO AND COCOA POWDER

I have used both these powders in the recipes. Cocoa powder has a sweeter and deeper chocolate flavour, which is delicious in baking, but cacao powder offers more health benefits. Being rich in flavonoids, fibre, potassium, iron and magnesium, and also containing protein, cacao can help reduce blood pressure and inflammation in the body, and lower the risk of diabetes. And because cacao powder is processed at much lower temperatures, it retains more of its nutritional value.

Either will work equally well. Just make sure you use a 100 per cent cocoa powder, as other cocoa or chocolate powders may not be vegan.

PLANT-BASED MILKS

These milks are really important when it comes to achieving a delicious texture. Make your own or use shop-bought varieties. I find that oat milk generally seems to work best in sponges, but you can use any plant-based milk you may have in the refrigerator.

PLAIN FLOUR

I have tried various flours for mug cakes, but plain seems to give the best results. Self-raising flour sometimes overreacted with the cake ingredients or didn't rise enough. Using plain flour and baking powder allows greater control over the use of the raising agent, giving a more consistent result.

VEGAN FATS

Vegetable oil, coconut oil and vegan spreads and butters all work well when cooked in the microwave. Vegetable oil is the easiest to blend with the ingredients, and because it's flavourless, it works with any flavour combination.

If you use a vegan butter, make sure it's softened so that you can beat it into the other ingredients thoroughly.

VEGAN DECORATIONS

Most cake decorations are not vegan-friendly and often contain egg. Plenty of suppliers online offer vegan alternatives. Whole food supermarkets and health-food shops also stock options. Check the ingredients on the packaging before using.

Before you begin...

MUGS

Depending on the recipe, I have specified using either a large mug, with a minimum capacity of 350ml (12fl oz), or a medium-sized mug, with a minimum capacity of 300ml (10fl oz). All the recipes serve one, unless stated otherwise. Using a larger mug will not affect the result, but with a smaller mug, the cake batter might overflow, and also over-cook, so you will need to use less batter. Don't fill the mug more than three-quarters full – you can use the excess to make an extra cake for a friend! Using less batter in a smaller mug will affect the cooking times – cook the cake initially for 1 minute 40 seconds at 600W, then cook it further in 20-second bursts, checking after each burst, until the cake is done (see page 12 for how to check that it's cooked).

Check that your chosen mug is safe to use in the microwave by looking for a little microwave sign on the base of the mug. If it doesn't have one, there is a chance that the mug could crack when heated in the microwave, or it could become very hot and scald you. If you are unsure, test the mug in the microwave for 1 minute on high: if the mug is boiling hot after this, it's not microwave-friendly, but if you can pick it up, it probably is. Make sure not to put any metal in the microwave, as it will spark and damage or break the microwave – and could cause an explosion.

I much prefer to make my cakes in a wider, thicker mug. I find that the sponge tends to cook a little better when it has a larger surface area, and is protected a little more by the thicker rim. And it also gives you more space for decoration!

MICROWAVE SETTINGS AND COOKING TIME

After extensive testing, I have found that vegan mug cakes work better when cooked on a lower microwave setting of 600W, so this is the only setting specified in the recipes. Your microwave may run at a higher wattage, and therefore a slight adjustment may be needed. If you are cooking the cake at 700–900W, cook initially for 2 minutes, and if after that time it has risen and feels set to the touch (see below), it's done. But if the cake sinks immediately, return it to the microwave and cook further in 20-second bursts, checking after each burst, until it's cooked. If your sponges are becoming quite hard or dry as they cool, this is because the cake is overcooked. Next time, reduce the cooking time by 20 seconds and see if the texture improves.

To check that your cake is cooked, gently press the top of the cake. The rise should hold and the cake should feel set. You can also test for doneness by inserting a skewer or cocktail stick into the centre of the cake: if it comes out clean with no uncooked batter attached, then the cake is done. The power levels of microwaves can vary, in the same way as the temperatures of ovens do. After you have made a few cakes, you will know if you need to adjust the cooking times slightly.

DOS AND DONT'S

Although mug cakes are very simple to make, every so often they can go a little wrong. So, for best results:

- **Don't** fill the mug more than three-quarters full. As tempting as it is, the batter will just dribble over the edges before it sets, leaving a sticky, cakey mess glued to the microwave – trust me, I've been there!

- **Do** put the mug on a plate in the microwave, which will save you hard work clearing up any mishaps.

- **Do** try again if your sponge turns out dry: try a larger mug and cook for 1 minute, then in 30-second bursts, checking if it's done after each burst. This will give you more control and prevent overcooking.

- **Don't** be disheartened if your cake sinks or doesn't look as pretty as you had hoped – it will still taste delicious, and gives you the more reason to make more mug cakes!

- **Don't** worry – before you know it, you will be the king or queen of the microwave mug cake!

Classics

Lemon & raspberry cake

2 tablespoons vegetable oil
2 tablespoons oat or almond milk
1½ tablespoons caster sugar
finely grated zest of ½ lemon
4½ tablespoons plain flour
½ teaspoon baking powder
1 tsp potato starch or cornflour
1 tbsp coconut yogurt
3 raspberries, plus extra to serve

For the icing
2 tablespoons icing sugar
½ teaspoon lemon juice

Lemon and raspberries are zingy, summery ingredients that make a great team. Fresh and simple, this cake is ideal for a little afternoon pick-me-up.

Mix together the oil, milk, caster sugar and lemon zest in a large mug. Add the flour, baking powder, potato starch or cornflour, and coconut yogurt, and mix well.

Drop in the raspberries, then wipe the rim of the mug clean of any cake batter. Microwave at 600W for 2 minutes 20 seconds.

Leave the cake to cool completely.

For the icing, mix the ingredients together in a small bowl until smooth, then drizzle over the cooled cake. Enjoy with extra raspberries.

Tip: *Try adding a teaspoon of raspberry jam to the top of the cake just before cooking.*

Coffee & walnut cake

If you are looking for the ultimate classic cake with a delectable coffee-infused vegan cream topping, look no further. Perfect if a friend or family member pops over for tea.

2 tablespoons vegan butter, softened
1½ tablespoons dark muscovado sugar
2 teaspoons instant coffee, dissolved
   in 1 tablespoon boiling water
4½ tablespoons plain flour
1 teaspoon potato starch or cornflour
½ teaspoon baking powder
2 tablespoons oat or almond milk
1 tablespoon coconut yogurt
1 tablespoon roughly chopped walnuts,
   plus extra to decorate

For the topping
3 tablespoons vegan double cream
½ tablespoon icing sugar
1 teaspoon instant coffee, dissolved
   in 1 tablespoon boiling water

In a large mug, beat together the butter, muscovado sugar and coffee until smooth. Add the flour, potato starch or cornflour, baking powder, milk, coconut yogurt and walnuts, and mix well.

Level the surface and wipe the frim of the mug clean of any cake batter, then microwave at 600W for 2 minutes 20 seconds.

Leave the cake to cool completely.

For the topping, put the ingredients into a small bowl and use a handheld electric mixer or balloon whisk to whip to soft peaks. Spoon or pipe onto the cooled cake and decorate with extra chopped walnuts.

Tip: *If walnuts are not your favourite, try swapping them for vegan chocolate chips or your nut of choice.*

Blueberry & almond swirl

If you love frangipane flavours, this is the cake for you. Try swapping the almond extract for another flavouring, such as coconut or orange extract.

2 tablespoons vegan butter, softened
2 tablespoons caster sugar
1 tablespoon blueberries
2 tablespoons almond milk
1 teaspoon almond extract
4½ tablespoons plain flour
1 teaspoon potato starch or cornflour
½ teaspoon baking powder

For the topping
3 tablespoons blueberries,
   plus extra to decorate
3 tablespoons icing sugar
5 tablespoons vegan cream cheese

Beat the butter and caster sugar together in a large mug until smooth. Stir in the blueberries, milk and almond extract, then add the flour, potato starch or cornflour and baking powder and mix well.

Level the surface and wipe the rim of the mug clean. Microwave at 600W for 2 minutes 20 seconds. Leave the cake to cool completely.

For the topping, put the blueberries into another mug and microwave at 600W for 1 minute until bubbling. Leave to stand for 5 minutes, then beat in 1 teaspoon of the icing sugar until smooth.

In a small bowl, beat the cream cheese with the remaining icing sugar until smooth and a little runny. Split the icing in half and mix 2 teaspoons of the blueberry coulis into one half. Put the white icing in one piping bag and the blueberry icing in another. Put a star nozzle in a large piping bag, then sit both filled piping bags inside the large bag. Pipe little stars all over the cake in your own pattern. Drizzle over the leftover coulis and top with a few extra berries.

Apple, olive oil & spice cake

½ Granny Smith apple, peeled, cored and finely diced
2 tablespoons light brown soft sugar
2 tablespoons olive oil
2 tablespoons almond milk
5 tablespoons plain flour
1 teaspoon potato starch or cornflour
½ teaspoon mixed spice
½ teaspoon baking powder
1 tablespoon coconut yogurt

For the icing
3 tablespoons vegan cream cheese
1½ tablespoons icing sugar
¼ teaspoon mixed spice

The olive oil and apple complement each other perfectly, making a lovely, gooey cake with a pleasing tang. I recommend using Granny Smith apples, but any apple will work.

Mix the apple, brown sugar, oil and milk together in a large mug. Cook in the microwave at 600W for 2 minutes.

Add the flour, potato starch or cornflour, mixed spice, baking powder and yogurt and mix well. Level the surface and wipe the rim of the mug clean of any cake batter, then microwave at 600W for 2 minutes 30 seconds.

Leave the cake to cool completely.

For the icing, beat the ingredients together in a small bowl, then spoon on top of the cooled cake.

Tip: *If you don't like mixed spice, you can simply leave it out, or try adding ½ teaspoon vanilla extract instead.*

Cinnamon & brown sugar sponge

Cinnamon and sugar always bring to mind comforting pastries or those wonderful hot doughnuts made fresh at the beach. I've captured that taste here, with the addition of sultanas (or raisins, if you only have those).

2 tablespoons vegetable oil
½ teaspoon ground cinnamon
2 tablespoons demerara sugar
4½ tablespoons plain flour
1 teaspoon potato starch or cornflour
½ teaspoon baking powder
1 teaspoon sultanas
1 tablespoon coconut yogurt
2 tablespoons almond or oat milk
vegan spray cream, to serve

For the topping
1 tablespoon demerara sugar
1 teaspoon sultanas or raisins

Mix the oil, cinnamon and sugar together in a large mug. Add the remaining cake ingredients, except the spray cream, and mix well. Level the surface and wipe the rim of the mug clean.

For the topping, mix the ingredients together in a small bowl. Sprinkle over the cake and microwave at 600W for 2 minutes 30 seconds.

Leave the cake to stand for a few minutes, then enjoy warm with a little vegan spray cream.

Tip: *Although the cake is best served warm with cream, if you let it cool, try a different topping: beat together 2 tablespoons icing sugar, 1 tablespoon softened vegan butter and a pinch of ground cinnamon, then spoon on top.*

Banana, choc & coconut cake

Banana and chocolate make a winning combination, and with the addition of coconut, this cake is unbeatable – especially when eaten warm!

1 small, ripe banana (no more than 80g/3oz), plus extra slices to serve (optional)
1½ tablespoons coconut oil
1½ tablespoons light brown soft sugar, plus extra to decorate
4 tablespoons plain flour
1 teaspoon potato starch or cornflour
½ teaspoon baking powder
2 tablespoons oat or almond milk
1 tablespoon coconut flakes
10g (¼oz) vegan dark chocolate, roughly chopped

Peel and roughly chop the banana, then place in a large mug with the coconut oil. Heat in the microwave at 600W for 1 minute, then stir.

Add the sugar, flour, potato starch or cornflour, baking powder and milk and mix well. Stir in half the coconut flakes and half the chocolate and level the surface, then sprinkle the remaining coconut flakes and chocolate over the top.

Wipe the rim of the mug clean of any cake batter, then microwave at 600W for 2 minutes 30 seconds.

Leave the cake to stand for 1 minute, then serve straight away, with extra slices of banana if you like.

Tip: *If your banana isn't very ripe, bash it in its skin before peeling and placing in the mug. This helps release its sugars.*

Sticky ginger & lime cake

finely grated zest of 1 lime
1 teaspoon lime juice
1 tablespoon stem ginger syrup
1½ tablespoons coconut oil
1 ball stem ginger, finely chopped
½ teaspoon baking powder
1½ tablespoons demerara sugar
¼ teaspoon ground ginger
4½ tablespoons plain flour
1 teaspoon potato starch
   or cornflour
1 tablespoon natural vegan
   or coconut yogurt
crystallised stem ginger,
   to serve (optional)

For the icing
3 tablespoons vegan cream cheese
2 teaspoons icing sugar
finely grated zest of ½ lime, plus extra to decorate

If ginger is your thing, then this cake is a must-try! The stem ginger syrup makes the sponge soft and nicely moist, and it has a little extra warming flavour from the ground ginger.

Put the lime zest and juice, ginger syrup and coconut oil into a large mug and heat in the microwave at 600W for 1 minute until the coconut oil has melted. Add the remaining cake ingredients, except the crystallised ginger, and mix well.

Level the surface and wipe the rim of the mug clean of any cake batter, then microwave at 600W for 2 minutes 30 seconds.

Leave the cake to cool completely.

For the icing, beat the ingredients together in a small bowl. Top the cake with the icing and then sprinkle over the extra lime zest, and some crystallised ginger, if using, to decorate.

Berry & pecan crumble cake

Crumble cakes offer an extra dimension of texture and taste, and are easier to make than you might expect. Although the microwave won't turn the crumble golden, it still tastes moreishly good!

2 tablespoons vegan butter, softened
2 tablespoons light brown soft sugar
1 tablespoon chopped pecans
1 tablespoon rolled oats
4 tablespoons plain flour
½ teaspoon baking powder
1 teaspoon potato starch or cornflour
1 tablespoon almond or oat milk
1 tablespoon coconut yogurt
2 tablespoons mixed berries, plus 3 berries
vegan spray cream or vegan custard, to serve

For the crumble topping
1 tablespoon rolled oats
1 tablespoon ground almonds
1 tablespoon vegan butter, softened
½ teaspoon light brown soft sugar

Beat the butter and sugar together in a large mug until smooth. Add all the remaining cake ingredients, except the 3 berries and spray cream or ice cream and mix well. Level the surface and wipe the rim of the mug clean.

For the crumble, mix the oats and ground almonds together in a bowl, then add the butter and rub it in with your fingertips. Stir through the sugar. Spoon the crumble on top of the cake batter and drop in the 3 berries.

Microwave at 600W for 2 minutes 30 seconds. Leave the cake to stand for 1 minute, then enjoy warm with some vegan spray cream or custard.

Tip: *You can use defrosted frozen berries if you can't get hold of fresh. Alternatively, try swapping the berries in the batter for raisins or diced apple.*

Spiced carrot cake

A satisfyingly gooey version of an enduring classic.

2 tablespoons grated carrot
2 tablespoons vegetable oil
1½ tablespoons dark muscovado sugar
3 tablespoons plain flour
1 teaspoon mixed spice
1 teaspoon potato starch or cornflour
½ teaspoon baking powder
2 tablespoons almond milk
1 tablespoon coconut yogurt

For the icing
1 tablespoon vegan cream cheese
1 tablespoon icing sugar
a little cinnamon, to decorate

Mix all the cake ingredients together in a large mug until well combined. Level the surface and wipe the rim of the mug clean, then microwave at 600W for 2 minutes 40 seconds. Leave the cake to cool completely.

For the icing, beat the cream cheese and icing sugar together in a small bowl until smooth. Top the cake with the icing and sprinkle with a little cinnamon to serve.

Tip: *Try using ground cinnamon instead of the mixed spice, and adding a teaspoon of sultanas.*

Peach Melba cake

I have used canned peaches here, but you can use fresh ripe peaches.

2 tablespoons vegetable oil
2 tablespoons caster sugar
2 canned peach halves, 1 finely chopped, 1 finely sliced
½ tablespoon peach syrup from the can
5 tablespoons plain flour
1 teaspoon potato starch or cornflour
½ teaspoon baking powder
1 tablespoon coconut yogurt
1 tablespoon oat milk
1 teaspoon vanilla extract
3 raspberries
vegan cream, to serve

In a large mug, mix together the oil, sugar, finely chopped peach, peach syrup, flour, potato starch or cornflour, baking powder, yogurt, milk and vanilla extract until well combined.

Level the surface and wipe the rim of the mug clean of any cake batter, then top with the sliced peach and the raspberries.

Microwave at 600W for 2 minutes 30 seconds.

Leave the cake to cool slightly, then serve with vegan cream.

Chocolate

Triple chocolate sponge

20g (¾oz) vegan dark chocolate
2 tablespoons coconut oil
2 tablespoons light brown soft sugar
1 tablespoon cocoa powder
4 tablespoons plain flour
½ teaspoon baking powder
1 teaspoon potato starch
   or cornflour
1 tablespoon coconut yogurt
1 tablespoon oat milk
10g (¼oz) vegan milk chocolate, chopped
10g (¼oz) vegan white chocolate,
   chopped, plus extra to decorate

For the ganache
20g (¾oz) vegan dark chocolate
10g (¼oz) vegan milk chocolate
3 tablespoons vegan double cream

For those chocoholic vegans out there, this cake will be your standout favourite! Try enjoying the cake warm, served with a scoop of vegan ice cream.

Put the dark chocolate, oil and sugar into a large mug and microwave at 600W for 2 minutes until the chocolate has melted, then stir. If it hasn't melted enough, heat further in 30-second bursts.

Add the remaining cake ingredients, reserving some of the milk chocolate and white chocolate, and mix well. Level the surface and wipe the rim of the mug clean. Top with the reserved milk chocolate and white chocolate, then microwave at 600W for 2 minutes 20 seconds. If not cooked through, microwave for a further 10 seconds. Leave to cool completely.

Add the chocolate for the ganache to another mug and heat in the microwave at 600W in 1-minute bursts, stirring after each burst, until it has melted. Quickly stir in the cream. Add a little extra cream if the ganache looks like it might split.

Spoon the ganache on top of the cooled cake and decorate with extra chopped white chocolate.

Peanut butter & chocolate cake

2 tablespoons vegetable oil
2 tablespoons light brown
   soft sugar
2 tablespoons peanut butter
25g (1oz) tablespoons vegan dark
   chocolate, roughly chopped,
   plus an extra grating to serve
4 tablespoons plain flour
1 teaspoon potato starch
   or cornflour
½ teaspoon baking powder
1 tablespoon coconut yogurt
1 tablespoon oat milk
vegan spray cream, to serve

Although peanut butter is not something I crave, I know how much others love it, so I called in a friend who assured me that this was peanutty enough!

Mix the oil, sugar and peanut butter together in a large mug until smooth. Add half the chopped chocolate, along with the flour, potato starch or cornflour, and baking powder and mix well. Stir in the yogurt and milk.

Level the surface and wipe the rim of the mug clean of any cake batter, then sprinkle the remaining chopped chocolate on top.

Microwave at 600W for 2 minutes 20 seconds.

Leave the cake to stand for 1 minute, then serve warm with vegan spray cream and a grating of chocolate.

Tip: *If, like me, you aren't the biggest fan of peanut butter, try this recipe using almond or cashew butter instead.*

Hazelnut & cacao cake

Hazelnut and cacao are always delicious together, and certainly work like a dream in this sponge, which is topped with a creamy, chocolatey icing for an indulgent treat.

2 tablespoons vegetable oil
2 tablespoons caster sugar
1 tablespoon cacao powder
½ tablespoon cacao nibs, plus extra to decorate
1 tablespoon hazelnuts, roughly chopped, plus extra, toasted, to decorate
4 tablespoons plain flour
½ teaspoon baking powder
1 teaspoon potato starch or cornflour
1 tablespoon oat or almond milk
10g (¼oz) vegan milk chocolate, chopped

For the icing
3 tablespoons vegan double cream
½ tablespoon cacao powder
½ tablespoon icing sugar

Mix all the cake ingredients together in a large mug until well combined.

Level the surface and wipe the rim of the mug clean of any cake batter, then microwave at 600W for 2 minutes 20 seconds.

Leave the cake to cool completely.

For the icing, whip the cream with a handheld electric mixer or balloon whisk in a small bowl to soft peaks. Add the cocoa powder and icing sugar and whisk into the cream.

Spoon the icing on top of the cooled cake. Sprinkle with the chopped toasted hazelnuts and cacao nibs.

Tip: *If you can get hold of a vegan chocolate and hazelnut spread, this will make a great alternative to the icing, along with a little extra vegan cream.*

Chocolate, pear & almond cake

Chocolate and pear make one of my all-time favourite combinations, and especially when you add almond into the mix. This cake is best enjoyed warm.

2 tablespoons vegetable oil
1 tablespoon vegan vanilla yogurt
2 tablespoons light brown soft sugar
1 tablespoon ground almonds
1 tablespoon oat milk
½ teaspoon baking powder
1 tablespoon cocoa powder
3 tablespoons plain flour
1 teaspoon potato starch or cornflour
20g (¾oz) vegan dark chocolate, roughly chopped
½ small ripe pear, peeled and cored, half chopped, half finely sliced
vegan cream or custard, to serve

Mix the oil, yogurt and sugar together in a large mug. Add the ground almonds, milk, baking powder, cocoa powder, flour and potato starch, and mix well.

Stir in most of the dark chocolate, along with the finely chopped pear. Level the surface and wipe the rim of the mug clean of any cake batter, then sprinkle over the remaining chocolate and top with the sliced pear.

Microwave at 600W for 2 minutes 30 seconds.

Leave the cake to stand for 1 minute, then serve warm with a spoonful of vegan cream or custard.

Matcha & white chocolate cake

Matcha powder can vary greatly in strength, so if you think yours smells particularly strong, try using a generous pinch the first time you make this, rather than ½ teaspoon.

2 tablespoons vegetable oil
2 tablespoons light brown soft sugar
1 tablespoon coconut yogurt
½ teaspoon matcha powder
1 tablespoon oat milk
½ teaspoon baking powder
4½ tablespoons plain flour
1 teaspoon potato starch or cornflour
30g (1oz) vegan white chocolate, roughly
    chopped, plus 10g (¼oz) for the topping

Mix the oil, sugar, yogurt and matcha together in a large mug. Add the remaining cake ingredients, reserving a little of the chocolate, and mix well. Level the surface and wipe the rim of the mug clean of any cake batter, then sprinkle the reserved chocolate on top.

Microwave at 600W for 2 minutes 30 seconds.

Leave the cake to stand while you make the topping.

Put the white chocolate for the topping into another mug and microwave at 600W in 30-second bursts, stirring after each burst, until the chocolate has melted.

Drizzle the white chocolate over the warm sponge and serve straight away.

Oreo brownie cake

In my opinion, Oreos are definitely one of the top shop-bought biscuits, and are a brownie's best friend. Wickedly moreish, you definitely won't want to share this cake!

2 tablespoons vegetable oil
2 tablespoons demerara sugar
2 tablespoons cocoa powder
3 tablespoons plain flour
1 tablespoon potato starch
  or cornflour
½ teaspoon baking powder
2 tablespoons oat or almond milk
10g (¼oz) vegan dark chocolate,
  roughly chopped
1 tablespoon coconut yogurt
2 Oreo cookies, roughly crumbled
vegan ice cream, to serve

Mix the oil, sugar and cocoa powder together in a large mug until smooth. Add the flour, potato starch or cornflour, baking powder, milk, chocolate and yogurt, and mix well.

Level the surface and wipe the rim of the mug clean of any cake batter, then press the crumbled Oreos into the batter.

Microwave at 600W for 2 minutes 30 seconds.

Leave the cake to stand for 1 minute, then enjoy warm with vegan ice cream.

Tip: You can switch the Oreos for any of your favourite vegan biscuits.

Chocolate lava cake

2 tablespoons vegetable oil
1 tablespoon coconut yogurt
2 tablespoons light brown soft sugar
1 tablespoon oat milk
4 tablespoons plain flour
1 tablespoon cocoa powder
1 teaspoon potato starch or cornflour
½ teaspoon baking powder
20g (¾oz) vegan dark chocolate,
   roughly chopped
2 tablespoons vegan chocolate spread
   or vegan chocolate and hazelnut spread
vegan ice cream, to serve

Who doesn't love chocolate lava cake? Because microwaves cook food from the inside out, I have used chocolate spread to keep the centre gooey and soft while the cake batter firms. Perfect with ice cream.

Mix the oil, yogurt, sugar and milk together in a small bowl until smooth. Add the flour, cocoa powder, potato starch or cornflour, baking powder and half the chocolate, and mix well.

Line a large mug with clingfilm as smoothly as possible. Sprinkle the remaining chopped chocolate into the bottom of the mug and then spoon in half the cake batter. Add the chocolate spread, then cover with the remaining batter and level the surface.

Microwave at 600W for 2 minutes.

Leave the cake to stand for 5 minutes, then carefully lift the warm cake out of the mug using the clingfilm. Invert on to a plate and remove the clingfilm. Serve with your favourite vegan ice cream.

Tip: *Try swapping the spread for peanut butter or roughly chopped vegan chocolate.*

Chocolate mint cake

2 tablespoons vegetable oil
2 tablespoons light brown soft sugar
3 tablespoons plain flour
1 teaspoon potato starch or cornflour
½ teaspoon baking powder
1 tablespoon cocoa powder
1 tablespoon plant milk
1 tablespoon coconut yogurt
20g (¾oz) vegan dark chocolate,
    roughly chopped, plus extra
    to decorate
1 teaspoon peppermint extract

For the icing
2 tablespoons icing sugar
1 tablespoon vegan butter,
    softened
1–2 drops of green food colouring
1 drop of peppermint extract
vegan sprinkles

Mint chocolates remind me of my childhood, when my mum would serve them with coffee after dinner parties. If you like mint chocolates, you'll love this cake! You could eat this warm with vegan cream instead of icing.

Beat the oil and sugar together in a large mug until smooth. Add the flour, potato starch or cornflour and baking powder and mix well, then stir in the remaining cake ingredients, reserving a little of the dark chocolate, and mix until combined.

Level the surface and wipe the rim of the mug clean of any cake batter. Sprinkle in the remaining chocolate, then microwave at 600W for 2 minutes 20 seconds.

Leave the cake to cool completely.

For the icing, beat the icing sugar and butter together with a wooden spoon in a small bowl until smooth, then beat in the colouring and flavouring.

Spoon the icing into a small piping bag fitted with a small piping nozzle. Swirl the icing on top of the cooled cake and add the vegan sprinkles.

Tip: *This recipe is easily turned into a chocolate orange cake by using the finely grated zest of ½ orange instead of the peppermint extract, and adding 1 teaspoon orange juice to the batter. Serve with orange segments and vegan cream instead of the icing.*

Pistachio & white chocolate cake

Pistachio cake is one of my favourites, especially when paired with white chocolate. I have kept this recipe simple, but it's well worth trying to find a good vegan pistachio ice cream to serve with it.

2 tablespoons vegetable oil
2 tablespoons caster sugar
4½ tablespoons plain flour
1 teaspoon potato starch
   or cornflour
½ teaspoon baking powder
1 tablespoon coconut yogurt
1 tablespoon plant milk
30g (1oz) vegan white chocolate,
   roughly chopped
2 tablespoons roughly chopped pistachios
vegan pistachio or vanilla ice cream,
   to serve

Mix the oil and sugar together in a large mug. Add the flour, potato starch or cornflour, baking powder, coconut yogurt and milk, along with half the chocolate and half the pistachios. Mix well.

Level the surface and wipe the rim of the mug clean of any cake batter, then sprinkle over the remaining chocolate and pistachios.

Microwave at 600W for 2 minutes 30 seconds.

Leave the cake to stand for a few minutes, then serve warm with vegan pistachio or vanilla ice cream.

Tip: *This cake is also delicious eaten cold, topped with a drizzle of melted white chocolate.*

Chocolate tahini cake

2 tablespoons vegetable oil
1 tablespoon coconut yogurt
2 teaspoons tahini
2 tablespoons light brown soft sugar
1 tablespoon oat milk
½ teaspoon baking powder
1 tablespoon cocoa powder
4 tablespoons plain flour
1 teaspoon potato starch
    or cornflour
20g (¾oz) vegan dark
    chocolate, roughly chopped

For the icing
1 tablespoon vegan butter,
    softened
1 tablespoon icing sugar
1 teaspoon tahini

Tahini and chocolate are great companions, so if you fancy trying something different, you won't be disappointed with this cake.

Mix the oil, yogurt and tahini together in a large mug. Add the remaining cake ingredients and mix well.

Level the surface and wipe the rim of the mug clean of any cake batter, then microwave at 600W for 2 minutes 30 seconds.

Leave the cake to cool completely.

For the icing, beat the ingredients together with a wooden spoon in a small bowl until smooth. Spoon on the top of the cooled cake and enjoy!

Desserts

Sticky toffee pudding

2 tablespoons finely chopped pitted dates
½ teaspoon bicarbonate of soda
2 tablespoons almond milk
1 teaspoon flaxseeds
2 tablespoons dark muscovado sugar
2 tablespoons vegetable oil
4 tablespoons plain flour
½ teaspoon baking powder
vegan vanilla ice cream,
  to serve

For the caramel sauce
3 tablespoons dark
  muscovado sugar
6 tablespoons vegan
  double cream
2 tablespoons vegan butter

A classic pudding that is guaranteed to satisfy any sweet cravings. This recipe makes plenty of caramel, so if you have any left over, store it in the fridge for up to 1 week.

Begin with the caramel sauce. Gently heat the ingredients in a small saucepan over a low heat, stirring until the butter has melted and the sugar has dissolved. Increase the heat to medium, bring to a simmer and whisk until the caramel thickens and turns a deep golden brown (about 5 minutes). If it splits, keep whisking and drizzle in a little more cream. Leave to cool.

Put the dates, bicarbonate of soda and milk into a large mug and microwave at 600W for 1 minute. Add the remaining pudding ingredients, along with 1 tablespoon of the caramel sauce, and mix well. Level the surface and wipe the rim of the mug clean of any batter, then microwave at 600W for 2 minutes 30 seconds. Leave to stand for 2 minutes while you warm through the sauce.

Top the pudding with a scoop of vegan ice cream and a generous drizzle of the sauce, and serve.

Apple & cinnamon cake

½ Granny Smith apple, peeled and
   cored, half diced, half sliced
2½ tablespoons dark muscovado sugar
2 tablespoons vegetable oil
4 tablespoons plain flour
1 teaspoon potato starch
   or cornflour
1 tablespoon coconut yogurt
½ teaspoon baking powder
¼ teaspoon ground cinnamon,
   plus extra to serve
1 tablespoon almond milk
vegan spray cream, to serve

Warm homemade apple pie is always a winner, but for those occasions when you don't have the time to make one, this speedy cake alternative will definitely hit the spot!

Put the diced apple into a large mug with 1 teaspoon of the sugar. Cook in the microwave at 600W for 1 minute.

Add the remaining ingredients, except the sliced apple, and mix well. Level the surface and wipe the rim of the mug clean of any cake batter, then arrange the sliced apple on top. Microwave at 600W for 2 minutes 30 seconds.

Leave the cake to stand for 1 minute, then serve warm with vegan spray cream and a little sprinkle of cinnamon.

Tip: *If you don't like cinnamon, you can simply omit it, or try adding ½ teaspoon vanilla extract and 10g (¼oz) roughly chopped vegan dark chocolate.*

Vanilla chai cake

2 tablespoons vegetable oil
2 tablespoons light brown soft sugar
1 tablespoon coconut yogurt
4 tablespoons plain flour
1 teaspoon potato starch
   or cornflour
½ teaspoon baking powder
¼ teaspoon ground cardamom
¼ teaspoon ground cinnamon
¼ teaspoon ground allspice
⅛ teaspoon ground cloves
1 teaspoon vanilla extract
2 tablespoons oat or almond
   milk

To serve
½ tablespoon icing sugar
vegan cream or ice cream

This is such a simple recipe, but the mix of spices makes it a warming and flavourful treat.

Mix all the cake ingredients together in a large mug until smooth.

Level the surface and wipe the rim of the mug clean of any batter. Microwave at 600W for 2 minutes 30 seconds.

Leave to stand for a few minutes, then sift over the icing sugar. Enjoy warm with a spoonful of vegan cream or a scoop of vegan ice cream.

Tip: *If you don't have all the spices listed, don't worry – just use the ones you do have. If you only want to buy a couple of spices, I would suggest using cardamom and cinnamon.*

Coconut & lemon cake

2 tablespoons coconut oil
2 tablespoons coconut milk
1 tablespoon coconut yogurt
2 tablespoons demerara sugar
1 tablespoon desiccated coconut
4 tablespoons plain flour
1 teaspoon potato starch or cornflour
½ teaspoon baking powder
1 teaspoon coconut extract
finely grated zest of ½ lemon, plus extra to serve
vegan yogurt, to serve

Put the coconut oil into a large mug and heat in the microwave at 600W for 1 minute 30 seconds until it has melted.

Add the remaining cake ingredients and mix well. Level the surface and wipe the rim of the mug clean of any cake batter, then microwave at 600W for 2 minutes 30 seconds.

Leave to stand for 5–10 minutes, then serve warm with vegan yogurt and extra lemon zest.

Tip: *This is equally delicious cold – try swirling a spoonful of raspberry jam through coconut yogurt to top the cooled cake.*

Coconut and lemon make the perfect flavour pairing for vegan sponges. The coconut oil and coconut milk keep the sponge perfectly moist. Lime zest would also work well here instead of the lemon.

Turmeric, ginger & orange cake

In addition to its health benefits, turmeric offers a vibrant colour and a fragrant flavour that works brilliantly with ginger and orange. **If you fancy trying something a little out of the ordinary, this is the dessert for you.**

2 tablespoons vegetable oil
2 tablespoons light brown soft sugar
4 tablespoons plain flour
1 tablespoon ground almonds
1 teaspoon potato starch or cornflour
1 tablespoon coconut yogurt
½ teaspoon baking powder
1 tablespoon oat or almond milk
¼ teaspoon ground turmeric
¼ teaspoon ground ginger
1 teaspoon finely grated orange zest
1 satsuma slice or ¼ orange slice
coconut yogurt, to serve

Mix together all the cake ingredients, except the satsuma or orange slice, in a large mug until well combined.

Level the surface and wipe the rim of the mug clean of any cake batter, then place the satsuma slice or piece of orange on top.

Microwave at 600W for 2 minutes 30 seconds.

Leave the cake to cool for 10 minutes, then serve slightly warm with a spoonful of coconut yogurt.

Blackberry & lime upside-down cake

2 tablespoons vegetable oil
2 tablespoons caster sugar
finely grated zest of 1 lime
juice of ½ lime
4 tablespoons plain flour
1 teaspoon potato starch
   or cornflour
½ teaspoon baking powder
1 tablespoon coconut yogurt
1 tablespoon blackberry jam

To serve
vegan cream or warm vegan custard
blackberries

Zingy lime teamed with tart blackberries and soft, sweet cake is a recipe for success, especially when served with vegan custard. You may need to stop other people from stealing a bite of this one!

Mix together all the cake ingredients, except the jam, in a small bowl until smooth.

Line a large mug with clingfilm as smoothly as possible. Spoon the jam into the bottom of the lined mug. Pour over the batter and level the surface.

Microwave at 600W for 2 minutes 30 seconds.

Leave the cake to stand for 5 minutes, then carefully lift the hot sponge out of the mug using the clingfilm. Invert it on to a plate and remove the clingfilm. Serve with vegan cream or warm vegan custard and blackberries.

Tip: *This recipe works really well with different fruit jams, especially blueberry or raspberry. Alternatively, finely grate the zest of ½ orange, then peel and segment the fruit and arrange a few orange segments in the bottom of the mug. Use the zest, plus the juice of ¼ of the orange instead of the lime in the batter.*

Key lime cake

Key lime pie is one of my favourite desserts, so I have used its flavours here, adding gingernut biscuits to the top as an alternative to the biscuit base.

2 tablespoons coconut oil
2 tablespoons coconut milk
2 tablespoons light brown soft sugar
1 tablespoon vegan cream cheese
finely grated zest of 1 lime
4 tablespoons plain flour
1 teaspoon potato starch or cornflour
½ teaspoon baking powder
2 gingernut biscuits, crumbled,
   plus extra to serve

For the icing
finely grated zest of ½ lime
3 tablespoons vegan cream cheese
2 tablespoons icing sugar

Put the coconut oil in a large mug and heat in the microwave at 600W for 2 minutes until it has melted.

Add all the remaining cake ingredients, except the gingernuts, and mix well. Level the surface and wipe the rim of the mug clean of any cake batter, then scatter over the crumbled gingernuts. Microwave at 600W for 2 minutes 30 seconds.

Leave the cake to cool completely.

For the icing, reserve a little of the lime zest to decorate, then beat the remainder into the cream cheese, along with the icing sugar, in a small bowl.

Spoon the icing on top of the cooled cake, then sprinkle over the reserved lime zest and scatter over some more crumbled gingernuts.

Tip: *If you don't have limes, lemons will also work well in this recipe.*

Vanilla, rose, berry & coconut cake

1 tablespoon vegetable oil
1 tablespoon caster sugar
2 tablespoons plain flour
½ teaspoon potato starch
  or cornflour
¼ teaspoon baking powder
½ tablespoon coconut yogurt
½ teaspoon rose extract
1 tablespoon berry jam (see tip)

For the topping
3 tablespoons vegan
  double cream
1 tablespoon icing sugar
2 tablespoons vegan custard
½ teaspoon vanilla extract
a few drops of rose extract
4 tablespoons mixed berries

My take on the traditional trifle, this sumptuous dessert is layered up with jam, custard, berries and vegan cream. The rose extract adds a lovely flavour, but you can use coconut extract instead.

Mix together all the cake ingredients except the jam in a large mug, preferably a glass one, until smooth. Level the surface and wipe the rim of the mug clean, then microwave at 600W for 1 minute, or until the cake has set. Leave to cool completely.

For the topping, put the cream and icing sugar into a small bowl and use a handheld electric mixer or balloon whisk to whip to soft peaks. Remove half the whipped cream and reserve for later, then add the custard and flavourings to the remaining whipped cream, and whip again to soft peaks.

Spread the jam in a layer on top of the cooled sponge, then add most of the creamy custard. Top with half the berries, then spoon over the reserved plain whipped cream. Top with the remaining berries. Enjoy straight away, or leave for up to 5 hours before eating.

Tip: *Use your favourite jam, and mix up the fruit depending on what's available. You could also add 20g (¾oz) fresh coconut with the berries.*

Cherry frangipane cake

2 tablespoons vegetable oil
2 tablespoons demerara sugar
4 tablespoons plain flour
1 tablespoon ground almonds
1 teaspoon potato starch
   or cornflour
½ teaspoon baking powder
2 tablespoons oat or almond milk
1 tablespoon coconut yogurt
½ teaspoon almond extract
2 cherries, halved and pitted,
   plus extra to serve
vegan double cream, to serve

This is a wonderful summertime special and delicious enjoyed warm with lashings of vegan cream. If cherries aren't your favourite fruit, try it with raspberries or blueberries.

Mix the oil and sugar together in a large mug. Add all the remaining cake ingredients, except the cherries, and mix well.

Level the surface and wipe the rim of the mug clean, then top with the cherry halves, cut-side down.

Microwave at 600W for 2 minutes 30 seconds.

Leave the cake to stand for 5 minutes, then serve warm with a few extra cherries and some vegan cream.

Biscoff spiced cake

2 tablespoons vegetable oil
2 tablespoons dark muscovado sugar
2 tablespoons Biscoff spread
4 tablespoons plain flour
1 teaspoon potato starch
   or cornflour
½ teaspoon baking powder
2 tablespoons almond milk
1 tablespoon coconut yogurt
1 Biscoff biscuit, crumbled

For the topping
1 tablespoon Biscoff spread
1 tablespoon vegan cream
1 Biscoff biscuit

For all the lovers of Lotus Biscoff out there, this one's for you. It was a wonderful day when I realised that they made a spread which is vegan, so I created this recipe in celebration!

Mix together all the cake ingredients, except the biscuit, in a large mug until well combined.

Level the surface and wipe the rim of the mug clean, then scatter the crumbled biscuit over the top.

Microwave at 600W for 2 minutes 30 seconds.

Leave the cake to cool completely.

For the topping, mix the Biscoff spread and cream together in a bowl. Spoon on top of the cooled cake and insert the biscuit, then enjoy straight away.

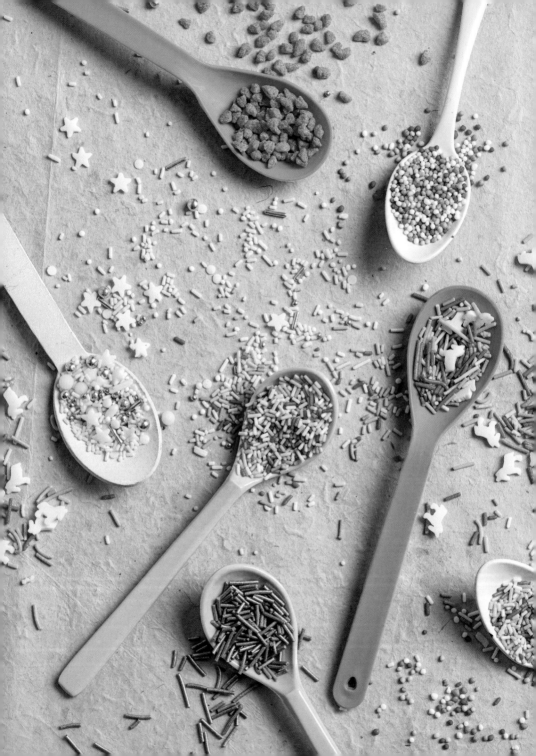

Celebrations

Lemon & strawberry birthday cake

We don't always want a big birthday cake; sometimes a little confection is all that's needed to make the day special. A lemon sponge is suitably celebratory, especially topped with sprinkles, glitter and a candle!

2½ tablespoons vegetable oil
1½ tablespoons granulated sugar
finely grated zest of ½ lemon
4½ tablespoons plain flour
1 teaspoon potato starch or cornflour
½ teaspoon baking powder
2 tablespoons almond milk
1 tablespoon coconut yogurt

For the filling & topping
3 tablespoons vegan double cream
1½ tablespoons icing sugar
2 strawberries, finely sliced

To decorate (optional)
vegan sprinkles and edible glitter
candle

Mix all the cake ingredients together in a small bowl until well combined. Line a large mug with clingfilm as smoothly as possible. Carefully pour the cake batter into the lined mug and level the surface. Microwave at 600W for 2 minutes 30 seconds, then leave to cool completely.

For the filling and topping, put the cream and icing sugar into a small bowl and use a handheld electric mixer or balloon whisk to whip to soft peaks.

Lift the cake out of the mug using the clingfilm. Cut in half horizontally and place a few strawberry slices on the bottom half, then spoon over one-third of the whipped cream. Cover with the top cake half and spoon over the remaining cream. Decorate with one strawberry slice, along with the vegan sprinkles and edible glitter. Finish with the candle and serve.

Tip: Try mixing up the fruits you use to fill and top your cake – blueberries and raspberries work well, or go for pineapple and passion fruit.

Rainbow birthday cake

2 tablespoons vegetable oil
2 tablespoons caster sugar
1 tablespoon coconut yogurt
½ teaspoon baking powder
¼ teaspoon bicarbonate of soda
5 tablespoons plain flour
1 teaspoon potato starch
   or cornflour
1 tablespoon oat milk
1 teaspoon vanilla extract
a few drops each of 4 different food
   colouring pastes (or add enough
   to make your preferred colour)

To serve
vegan spray cream
vegan sprinkles
candle

Everyone wants colour and fun on their birthday, and this cake really delivers! Choose your favourite combination of colours for the sponge layers – I find that paste colourings work best.

Stir together the oil, sugar and yogurt in a bowl until well combined. Add the remaining cake ingredients, except the food colouring, and mix well.

Divide the batter between 4 small bowls and stir a different food colouring into each. Spoon the first coloured batter into the bottom of a large glass mug and spread in an even layer. Repeat with the remaining colours, levelling each layer as you go.

Wipe the rim of the mug clean of any batter, then microwave at 600W for 2 minutes 30 seconds. Leave to cool completely.

Top with vegan spray cream and sprinkles. Finish with the candle and serve.

Tip: If you like, you can serve this warm. Just leave to stand for 5 minutes, then top and enjoy.

Valentine's red velvet

2 tablespoons vegetable oil
2 tablespoons light brown soft sugar
3 tablespoons plain flour
1 tablespoon cocoa powder
1 teaspoon potato starch or cornflour
½ teaspoon baking powder
1 tablespoon coconut yogurt
1 tablespoon oat or almond milk
½ teaspoon red paste food colouring

For the topping
3 tablespoons vegan cream cheese
1 tablespoon icing sugar

edible vegan heart sprinkles, to decorate

Mix all the cake ingredients together in a large mug until well combined.

Level the surface and wipe the rim of the mug clean of any cake batter, then microwave at 600W for 2 minutes 30 seconds.

For the icing, beat the vegan cream cheese and icing sugar together in a small bowl, then spoon on top of the cooled cake and scatter over the sprinkles. The cake is best eaten warm.

Red velvet cake is the perfect choice for Valentine's Day, and this easy yet delicious mug version will definitely send your true love the right message. You might have to make two, though...

Dark choc & raspberry cake for two

The perfect pairing of ingredients for celebrating with the one you love. And it must be real love if you can bring yourself to share this luxurious cake!

20g (¾oz) vegan dark chocolate
2 tablespoons vegetable oil
2 tablespoons caster sugar
½ teaspoon baking powder
1 teaspoon potato starch
   or cornflour
2 tablespoons cocoa powder
4 tablespoons plain flour
1½ tablespoons coconut yogurt
1½ tablespoons oat milk

To serve
vegan ice cream
raspberries
vegan chocolate sauce

Put the chocolate, oil and sugar into a large mug and microwave at 600W for 2 minutes, then stir. If the chocolate hasn't melted enough, return to the microwave and heat further in 30-second bursts, stirring after each burst, until completely melted.

Add the remaining cake ingredients and mix until smooth. Level the surface and wipe the rim of the mug clean of any cake batter, then microwave at 600W for 2 minutes 30 seconds.

Leave the cake to stand for 1 minute, then top with a generous scoop of vegan ice cream and some raspberries. Add a good drizzle of chocolate sauce and serve straight away.

Easter bunny cake

2 tablespoons vegetable oil
2 tablespoons light brown soft sugar
4½ tablespoons plain flour
1 teaspoon potato starch
    or cornflour
½ teaspoon baking powder
1 teaspoon mixed spice
1 tablespoon coconut yogurt
1 tablespoon oat milk

To decorate
100g (3½oz) vegan ready-to-roll green fondant icing
small quantity of vegan ready-to-roll white, black,
    pink, orange and green icing

Instead of mixed spice, try adding a tablespoon of vegan chocolate chips to the cake batter.

Mix the cake ingredients together in a small bowl until smooth. Line a large mug with clingfilm. Spoon the batter into the lined mug and level the surface, then microwave at 600W for 2 minutes 30 seconds. Leave to cool completely, then carefully lift the cake out of the mug using the clingfilm. Discard the clingfilm and place the cake flat-side down on a plate.

Roll out the green icing and use it to cover the cake, trimming the excess. Shape 2 small balls of white icing into bunny ears. Shape 2 smaller pieces of pink icing into rough triangle, then wet the ears with a little water and press a pink triangle onto the centre of each. Leave to dry for 30 minutes to 1 hour.

Use the black icing to make eyes and eyebrows, then make a nose with pink and paws with white. Use a cocktail stick to mark claws on the paws. Shape the orange icing into carrots and use a little more green for the tops. Use a little water to stick them in place, then serve.

Chocolate orange pumpkin

1 large whole orange, plus finely
   grated zest of 1 large orange
2 tablespoons vegetable oil
1½ tablespoons light brown soft sugar
3 tablespoons plain flour
1 tablespoon cocoa powder
1 teaspoon potato starch or cornflour
½ teaspoon baking powder
1 tablespoon coconut yogurt
1 tablespoon almond milk

Use a knife to cut off the top of the orange and set aside. Cut around the inside of the orange, between the white pith and flesh, and scoop out the flesh. Cut out eyes, a nose and a mouth on one side of the orange.

Mix the remaining ingredients together in a small bowl until well combined. Spoon the batter into the orange, filling it no more than three-quarters full. Microwave at 600W for 2 minutes. If it hasn't set, microwave in 10 second bursts.

Leave to cool completely, then replace the 'lid' of the orange to finish the 'pumpkin'.

Tip: *Try carving different patterns into the orange, or, if you are short of time, use a permanent marker to draw features on the orange after cooking instead.*

Instead of using a mug, I hollowed out and carved an orange to look just like a spooky jack-o'-lantern. You may have to make a few, as others will want to steal yours!

Wicked witch's cauldron

Halloween is always the perfect excuse to have some fun baking, and this recipe is great to do with kids. You can choose any colour you want for the witch's broth – just make it look suitably scary!

2 tablespoons vegetable oil
2 tablespoons caster sugar
5 tablespoons plain flour
1 teaspoon potato starch
    or cornflour
½ teaspoon baking powder
2 tablespoons almond milk
1 tablespoon coconut yogurt
1 teaspoon vanilla extract
1 teaspoon green paste food colouring

For the topping
3 tablespoons icing sugar
2 tablespoons vegan butter, softened
black paste food colouring

sweets, to decorate

Mix all the cake ingredients together in a large mug until well combined.

Level the surface and wipe the rim of the mug clean of any cake batter, then microwave at 600W for 2 minutes 30 seconds.

Leave the cake to cool completely.

For the icing, beat the icing sugar, butter and food colouring together with a wooden spoon in a small bowl until smooth.

Spoon the icing into a small piping bag fitted with a small standard or star piping nozzle and pipe it around the edge of the mug, then decorate with the sweets.

Pumpkin cake

Here I have taken the classic American pie served at Thanksgiving and reinvented it in mug form. Great for brightening up any autumn or winter's day.

2 tablespoons vegetable oil
2 tablespoons light brown soft sugar
5 tablespoons plain flour
1 teaspoon potato starch or cornflour
¼ teaspoon bicarbonate of soda
½ teaspoon baking powder
1 teaspoon mixed spice
pinch of grated nutmeg, plus extra to serve
1½ tablespoons canned pumpkin purée
1 tablespoon coconut yogurt
1 vegan biscuit (see tip), crumbled
vegan spray cream, to serve

Mix together all the cake ingredients, except the biscuit, in a large mug until smooth.

Level the surface and wipe the rim of the mug clean of any cake batter, then scatter over the crumbled biscuit.

Microwave at 600W for 2 minutes 30 seconds.

Leave the cake to stand for 1 minute before serving warm, topped with vegan spray cream and a grating of nutmeg.

Tip: *A gingernut works well here.*

Santa's hat cake

2 tablespoons vegan butter, softened
2 tablespoons caster sugar
5 tablespoons plain flour
1 teaspoon potato starch or cornflour
½ teaspoon baking powder
pinch of ground cinnamon
1 tablespoon raisins
2 tablespoons almond milk
1 tablespoon coconut yogurt
1 teaspoon vanilla extract

To decorate
100g (3½oz) vegan ready-to-roll red fondant icing
50g (1¾oz) vegan ready-to-roll white fondant icing
vegan writing icing
icing sugar

'Tis the season for cake! This fun and festive design is sure to get you into the Christmas spirit.

Beat the butter and sugar together in a small bowl until smooth. Line a large mug with clingfilm as smoothly as possible. Add the remaining cake ingredients and mix well. Spoon the cake batter into the lined mug and level the surface, then microwave at 600W for 2 minutes 30 seconds.

Leave the cake to cool completely, then carefully lift it out of the mug using the clingfilm. Remove the clingfilm and place the cake flat-side down on a plate.

Roll out the red icing into a rough square about 10–12cm (4–4½ inches) larger than your cake on each side, then cut away one side to make a triangle. Wrap this around the cake to form a cone and secure by wetting the icing edges with a little water and pressing them together. Shape the cone to wrinkle it and fold it a little at the top, as shown in the photo.

Shape a third of the white icing into a small ball and stick to the top of the hat with a little water. Roll the remaining white icing into a long sausage. Wrap it around the base of the hat and secure with a little water. Dust with icing sugar for snow, then serve.

Spiced rum choc egglessnog

This warming spiced rum and chocolate nog has all the flavour but none of the egg. Topped with vegan cream and brownie pieces, it makes a fitting treat for Christmas Eve.

For the brownie
1 tablespoon vegetable oil
1 tablespoon light brown soft sugar
2 tablespoons plain flour
2 teaspoons cocoa powder
¼ teaspoon baking powder
1 tablespoon almond milk
½ tablespoon coconut yogurt
10g (¼oz) vegan dark chocolate

For the choc nog
2 teaspoons cocoa powder
1 teaspoon light brown soft sugar
pinch of grated nutmeg
1 tablespoon rum or your favourite spirit
250ml (9fl oz) almond milk

To serve
vegan spray cream
vegan chocolate sauce (optional)

Mix together all the brownie ingredients, except the chocolate, in a small bowl. Line a medium-sized mug with clingfilm. Spoon the batter into the lined mug, level the surface, then top with the chocolate. Microwave at 600W for 1 minute 30 seconds.

Leave to cool for a few minutes, then lift out of the mug using the clingfilm. Discard the clingfilm and set the brownie aside.

Mix together the cocoa powder, sugar and nutmeg in a large clean mug. Stir in the rum, followed by the milk. Microwave at 600W for 1 minute. Stir and remove from the microwave, or heat for a further 30 seconds if you prefer it hotter.

Dice the brownie, then serve the hot choc nog, topped with vegan spray cream, the brownie pieces and vegan chocolate sauce.

Index

UK/US glossary

balloon whisk / wire whisk

bicarbonate of soda / baking soda

biscuit / cookie

caster sugar / superfine sugar

clingfilm / plastic wrap

cocktail stick / toothpick

crystallised stem ginger / candied preserved ginger

dark muscovado sugar / dark brown sugar

gingernut biscuits / gingersnaps

golden caster sugar / superfine sugar

icing / frosting

icing sugar / confectioners' sugar

jam / jelly

light brown soft sugar / light brown sugar

mixed spice / pumpkin pie spice

piping bag / pastry bag

piping nozzle / piping tip

plain flour / all-purpose flour

self-raising flour / self-rising flour

stem ginger / preserved ginger

sultanas / golden raisins

sweets / candy

vegan dark chocolate / vegan bittersweet chocolate

vegan double cream / vegan heavy cream

vegan natural yogurt / vegan plain yogurt

About the author

Lottie Covell is a freelance food stylist and recipe developer. She was previously Food and Lifestyle Editor for *delicious* magazine. She started working in recipe development and food styling after finishing her diploma course at Leith's School of Food and Wine. She wrote the recipes for *The Toblerone Cookbook*. Some of her clients include *Olive* Magazine, *Tesco* magazine, Slimming World, Marks & Spencer, *Sainsbury's* magazine and *BBC Good Food* magazine.

Acknowledgements

I think the best place to start is a big thank you to the team as a whole for bringing the vegan mug cake book together at an impressive rate! Thank you very much to everyone at Kyle Books who helped make the book as fun and colourful as you see it.

A big thank you to Judith, Jenny and Allison for all your help and making the book happen! It certainly wouldn't have come together in the way it has without all your advice, help and insight.

To Faye, thank you for all the lovely props, you really have made the cakes shine in all the wonderful array of patterns and colours!

Thank you, Tamin, for your brilliant photographs and enthusiasm for all 40 mug cakes!

Nikki, your design has brought the book together and made it look as fantastic as you can all see, so thank you very much.

Thank you to Ant, who tried and tasted a lot of the mug cakes and put up with 2 microwaves beeping in the kitchen for a number of weeks!

Finally, thank you to Alice, for all your help on the shoots. I was very grateful to have an extra pair of very capable hands!